MW00512859

False Claims Act & Qui Tam

Quarterly Review

Volume 91 • January 2019
Edited by Jacklyn DeMar
Taxpayers Against Fraud
TAF Education Fund

ISBN 978-0-9992185-9-4

Published by
Taxpayers Against Fraud
TAF Education Fund
1220 19th Street NW, Suite 501
Washington, DC 20036
Phone (202) 296-4827
Fax (202) 296-4838

Printed in the United States of America

The *False Claims Act and Qui Tam Quarterly Review* is published by the Taxpayers Against Fraud Education Fund ("TAFEF"). This publication provides an overview of major False Claims Act and *qui tam* developments including case decisions, DOJ interventions, and settlements.

The TAFEF is a nonprofit charitable organization dedicated to combating fraud against the government through the promotion and use of the *qui tam* provisions of the False Claims Act ("FCA"). The TAFEF serves to inform and educate the general public, the legal community, and other interested groups about the FCA and its *qui tam* provisions.

The TAFEF is based in Washington, D.C., where it maintains a comprehensive FCA library for public use and a staff of lawyers and other professionals who are available to assist anyone interested in the False Claims Act and *qui tam*.

TAF Education Fund

Taxpayers Against Fraud Education Fund
1220 19th Street NW
Suite 501
Washington, DC 20036
Phone (202) 296-4826
Fax (202) 296-4838
www.taf.org

TABLE OF CONTENTS

Anil J. Desai, M.D., East Metro Internal Medicine, LLC, and Rockdale-Newton Hematology-Oncology (N.D. Ga. Dec. 5, 2018)

ev3 Inc., Covidien LP (D. Mass., C.D. Cal. Dec. 4, 2018)

Rosicki, Rosicki & Associates, P.C. (S.D. N.Y. Dec. 4, 2018)

SK Energy Co. Ltd., GS Caltex Corp., Hanjin Transportation Co. Ltd. (S.D. Ohio Nov. 14, 2018)

Shaw University (E.D. N.C. Nov. 12, 2018)

British Airways and Iberia Airlines (Nov. 12, 2018)

Dandrow's Painting, Inc. (N.D. N.Y. Nov. 7, 2018)

Maryland Treatment Centers (D. M.D. Nov. 7, 2018)

ImmediaDent of Indiana, LLC (W.D. Ky. Nov. 6, 2018)

Northrop Grumman Systems Corporation (S.D. Cal. Nov. 2, 2018)

FROM THE EDITOR

As 2018 comes to an end, let us look back at trends that have emerged and notable recoveries. According to the Department of Justice's year-end press release, the government recovered $2.8 billion as a result of False Claims Act actions in the past year.[1] This total is slightly down from 2017, but enforcement efforts remained strong, with relators filing 645 *qui tam* actions and the DOJ bringing 122 actions. As in years past, *qui tam* actions made up a substantial majority of FCA cases resolved, and relators received awards of over $300 million as a result.[2]

Not surprisingly, health care fraud made up a significant majority of the cases, with $2.5 of the $2.8 billion in recoveries stemming from matters involving drug and medical device manufacturers, managed care providers, hospitals, pharmacies, hospice organizations, laboratories, and physicians. One standout was the *qui tam* action brought against AmerisourceBergen Corporation, which paid $625 million to settle claims that it "improperly repackaged oncology-supportive injectable drugs into pre-filled syringes and improperly distributed those syringes to physicians treating vulnerable cancer patients," and paid physicians kickbacks to induce them to prescribe AmerisourceBergen's drugs, causing false claims to be submitted to government-funded healthcare programs.[3] In addition to this and many other cases against drug and medical device manufacturers, there have been several cases involving Physician Assistance Programs (PAPs). On their face, PAPs are designed to provide financial assistance to provide needy patients with access to drugs for little or no cost, but these programs are often sponsored by pharmaceutical companies, and these relationships can lead to fraud and abuse. For instance, during the past fiscal year, United Therapeutics Corporation paid $210 million to settle allegations that it disguised kickbacks as charitable donations to a PAP in order to induce it to cover the costs of copayments for Medicare patients taking its drugs.[4] We expect to see more cases involving these organizations going forward.

Procurement fraud was another area of focus in 2018. One notable case involved allegations that Japanese manufacturer Toyobo Company and its U.S.-based subsidiary sold defective Zylon fiber used in manufacturing bullet proof vests provided to federal, state, local, and tribal law enforcement agencies. The *qui tam* action alleged that Toyobo knew that Zylon degraded quickly in normal heat and humidity and that this degradation rendered vests containing Zylon unfit for use, but actively continued

---

1. Justice Department Recovers Over $2.8 Billion from False Claims Act Cases in Fiscal Year 2018, available at https://www.justice.gov/opa/pr/justice-department-recovers-over-28-billion-false-claims-act-cases-fiscal-year-2018.

2. Department of Justice Fraud Statistics, available at https://www.justice.gov/civil/page/file/1080696/download?utm_medium=email&utm_source=govdelivery.

3. AmerisourceBergen Corporation Agrees to Pay $625 Million to Resolve Allegations That It Illegally Repackaged Cancer–Supportive Injectable Drugs to Profit From Overfill, available at https://www.justice.gov/opa/pr/amerisourcebergen-corporation-agrees-pay-625-million-resolve-allegations-it-illegally?utm_medium=email&utm_source=govdelivery.

4. United Therapeutics Agrees to Pay $210 Million to Resolve Allegations that it Paid Kickbacks Through a Co-Pay Assistance Foundation, available at https://www.justice.gov/usao-ma/pr/united-therapeutics-agrees-pay-210-million-resolve-allegations-it-paid-kickbacks-through?utm_medium=email&utm_source=govdelivery.

to market and sell the fiber to the government.[5] Toyobo agreed to pay $66 million to resolve the claims.

There were also several settlements involving the importation of goods and alleged evasion of customs duties, including a $10.5 million settlement with the Bassett Mirror Company. The *qui tam* complaint alleged that Bassett evaded antidumping duties on wooden bedroom furniture imported from China by knowingly misclassifying the furniture as non-bedroom furniture on its official import documents.[6]

The government and relators continued to pursue individual defendants in 2018, and that trend will likely continue. Among several cases involving individual defendants, the DOJ settled *qui tam* claims with Prime Healthcare Services and its Chief Executive Officer, Dr. Prem Reddy, who agreed to pay $65 million, including $3,250,000 from Reddy individually, to resolve allegations that they engaged in a deliberate scheme to increase medically unnecessary inpatient admissions of Medicare beneficiaries.[7]

On the other hand, the government seemed to pivot away from cases involving mortgage fraud this year. The only significant case that settled in 2018 involving mortgage loans in any way focused on allegations unrelated to the underlying mortgage fraud itself. Rather, the government brought FCA claims against Deloitte & Touche LLP alleging that the independent auditor knowingly deviated from applicable auditing standards and failed to detect another company's fraudulent scheme involving the purported sale of fictitious or double-pledged mortgage loans insured by the Federal Housing Administration. Deloitte agreed to pay $149.5 million to resolve the claims.[8]

We will continue to monitor the ups and downs of FCA enforcement, and hope you enjoy this volume and find it a useful resource for your practice and continuing legal education.

Sincerely,

Jacklyn N. DeMar, Esq.
Editor-in-Chief

---

5. Japanese Fiber Manufacturer to Pay $66 Million for Alleged False Claims Related to Defective Bullet Proof Vests, available at https://www.justice.gov/opa/pr/japanese-fiber-manufacturer-pay-66-million-alleged-false-claims-related-defective-bullet?utm_medium=email&utm_source=govdelivery.

6. Bassett Mirror Company Agrees to Pay $10.5 Million to Settle False Claims Act Allegations Relating to Evaded Customs Duties, available at https://www.justice.gov/opa/pr/bassett-mirror-company-agrees-pay-105-million-settle-false-claims-act-allegations-relating?utm_medium=email&utm_source=govdelivery.

7. Prime Healthcare Services and CEO to Pay $65 Million to Settle False Claims Act Allegations, available at https://www.justice.gov/opa/pr/prime-healthcare-services-and-ceo-pay-65-million-settle-false-claims-act-allegations?utm_medium=email&utm_source=govdelivery.

8. Deloitte & Touche Agrees to Pay $149.5 Million to Settle Claims Arising From Its Audits of Failed Mortgage Lender Taylor, Bean & Whitaker, available at https://www.justice.gov/opa/pr/deloitte-touche-agrees-pay-1495-million-settle-claims-arising-its-audits-failed-mortgage.

Recent False Claims Act & *Qui Tam* Decisions

NOVEMBER 1, 2018–DECEMBER 31, 2018

FALSE CLAIMS ACT LIABILITY

A. Procurement Fraud

U.S. ex rel. Gates v. United Airlines Inc., 912 F.3d 190 (4th Cir. Dec. 26, 2018)

> **Holding: The United States Court of Appeals for the Fourth Circuit affirmed the district court's decision granting the defendant's motion to dismiss the relator's procurement fraud claims for failure to plead fraud with particularity under Rule 9(b), but reversed the decision to dismiss the relator's retaliation claims.**

The relator brought a *qui tam* action against his former employer, United Airlines, which had a government subcontract to maintain engines for military transport planes, alleging that the defendant violated the False Claims Act by falsely certifying that it followed contractual requirements for repairs and inspections to the engines. Boeing, United's subcontractor, had been awarded an Air Force contract with an $11.75 billion umbrella payment, a portion of which was earmarked for the maintenance of the military planes. Relator alleged that United falsely certified that certain work had been completed, improperly certified repairs that had been made with uncalibrated tools, and allowed inspectors to continue certifying repairs after their training and eye exams had expired, all in violation of the terms of the contract. The relator alleged that he complained about the conduct to his supervisors on multiple occasions, warning that the defendant was violating the terms of the contract and stating that the violations could result in "catastrophic failure to an engine." He alleged that his employment was terminated shortly thereafter in violation of the FCA's retaliation provisions. The United States District Court for the District of South Carolina granted the defendant's motion to dismiss the relator's substantive fraud claims for failure to plead with particularity under Rule 9(b) and dismissed the relator's retaliation claims for failure to state a claim under Rule 12(b)(6). The relator appealed to the Fourth Circuit.

The circuit court, with one judge dissenting, upheld the district court's decision granting the defendant's motion to dismiss the substantive FCA claims, but reversed the dismissal of the retaliation claims. The court explained that, while the relator adequately pled that the defendant engaged in fraudulent conduct, he failed to allege how or whether the bills for the fraudulent services were presented to the government, or whether the government paid United for the services. The court observed that "merely alleging fraudulent conduct and an umbrella payment, without more, [was] insufficient particularly where…United [was] three levels removed from the Air Force, which contract[ed] directly with Boeing." The court indicated that the relator's allegations left open the possibility that the intervening contractors declined to bill the government for the repairs, that the government refused to pay, or that the fraudulent repairs were remedied prior to payment. The court explained that the relator was not required to produce documentation at the pleading stage, but was required to "connect the dots" between the false claims and government payment. However, the circuit court reversed the district court's decision on the retaliation claims, finding that the relator sufficiently alleged that he was engaged in protected activity with an objectively reasonable belief that the defendant was violating the FCA and that his actions were designed to stop the violations. The court also noted that the relator alleged sufficiently that the defendant knew about his protected conduct and terminated his employment because of that conduct. The dissenting judge agreed, and went on to state that she believed that the relator had stated his substantive FCA claims sufficiently to satisfy Rule 9(b).

U.S. ex rel. Mateski v. Raytheon Co., 745 Fed.Appx. 49 (9th Cir. Dec. 11, 2018)

> **Holding: The United States Court of Appeals for the Ninth Circuit affirmed the district court's decision granting the defendant's motion to dismiss the relator's procurement fraud claims for failure to plead fraud with particularity under Rule 9(b).**

The relator brought a *qui tam* action against the government contractor where he was formerly employed alleging that the defendant falsely certified compliance with the terms of its contract regarding testing related to a sensor for a satellite system. The United States District Court for the Central District of California granted the defendant's motion to dismiss, finding that the relator failed to meet the requirements of Rule 9(b) or to plead materiality sufficiently. The relator appealed to the Ninth Circuit.

The circuit court upheld the decision of the district court, explaining that the relator did not explain properly what tests the defendant failed to perform, on which components, and when the claims were submitted. Further, the court found that the relator failed to supply sufficient facts from which it could determine whether the contractual breaches were material.

U.S. ex rel. Fields v. Bi-State Dev. Agency, 2018 WL 5981943 (E.D. Mo. Nov. 14, 2018)

Holding: The United States District Court for the Eastern District of Missouri granted the defendant's motion for summary judgment on the relator's procurement fraud false certification claims, finding that the relator failed to provide evidence that a false claim was submitted.

The relator brought a *qui tam* action against the government contractor where he was formerly employed, alleging that the defendant falsely certified compliance with federal laws in order to receive federal public transit funds in violation of the False Claims Act. He alleged that defendant Bi-State falsified its compliance with the Hatch Act and Uniform Relocation Act, while violating those laws by requiring employees to support a local county executive's election campaign, instituting a "pay to play" scheme for political donors. Relator also alleged that Bi-State failed to appraise a parking garage before buying it at an inflated price from a company affiliated with the campaign, thereby violating the Anti-Kickback Statute. The defendant moved for summary judgment, arguing that the relator failed to adduce evidence that it actually presented false claims to the government or caused false claims to be presented.

The court granted the defendant's motion to dismiss. The court explained that the relator failed to produce evidence of any claims for payment or any certification of compliance with relevant laws made in connection with the receipt of grants from the federal government. The court noted that the only evidence presented was the relator's own testimony about the scheme, which was not sufficient to defeat a motion for summary judgment.

U.S. ex rel. Folliard v. Comstor Corp., 2018 WL 5777085 (D.D.C. Nov. 2, 2018)

Holding: The United States District Court for the District of Columbia denied relator's motion for reconsideration of the court's decision granting the defendants' motion to dismiss the his procurement fraud claims for failure to state a claim under Rule 12(b)(6).

The relator brought a *qui tam* action against a government contractor and its subsidiary, alleging that the defendants violated the False Claims Act by selling the government products that originated in non-designated countries in violation of the Trade Agreement Act (TAA), and falsely certifying that they were in compliance with the TAA. The court granted the defendants' motion to dismiss, finding that the relator failed to adequately plead falsity, materiality, or scienter under Rule 12(b)(6). The relator moved for reconsideration.

The court denied the relator's motion for reconsideration, finding that there was no clear prejudice to the relator or fundamental unfairness under governing law. The court found that the relator's allegations that the particular products at issue were required to comply with the TAA or actually violated the statute were conclusory. The court noted that the relator failed to cite any authority that the requirements under the contract included TAA compliance for those specific products. Further, the court found that the relator failed to plead materiality adequately because he alleged only that compliance with the TAA was explicitly identified as a condition of payment, but that this was not sufficient to allege materiality. The court rejected relator's argument that it had erred by affording weight to the government's decision not to intervene in the case, explaining that the court discussed intervention only in support of the conclusion that it had already reached that compliance was not material. Additionally, the court rejected relator's argument that the court assigned too much weight to relator's failure to plead that the government stopped payment or had done so in similar cases, explaining that "[n]ot pleading that the government cancelled defendants' contracts did not doom the relator's [complaint]...[but o]mitting any fact from which materiality could plausibly be inferred did." Finally, the court found that relator's scienter allegations were too conclusory.

B. Customs Fraud

U.S. ex rel. Schagrin v. LDR Indus., LLC, 2018 WL 6064699 (N.D. Ill. Nov. 20, 2018)

> **Holding: The United States District Court for the Northern District of Illinois granted the relator's motion for reconsideration, then granted the defendant's motion to dismiss the relator's customs fraud claims on Rule 9(b) grounds.**

The relator, an attorney experienced in the steel industry, brought a *qui tam* action against a steel manufacturer and importer and its owners, alleging that they misclassified pipe they imported in order to avoid paying customs duties in violation of the False Claims Act. The court granted the defendants' motion to dismiss pursuant to the government action bar, finding that the government's proof of claim in the defendants' bankruptcy case constituted the initiation of a penalty proceeding by the government, and that the relator's allegations were based on the same transactions as the government penalty proceeding. The relator moved for reconsideration and the government submitted declarations stating that the proceeding had not yet occurred and there had been no collection of money by the government. The court granted the relator's motion for reconsideration and reversed its original holding based on those declarations, but considered the defendant owners' alternative arguments for dismissal.

The court granted the motion to dismiss for failure to state a claim under Rule 12(b)(6), finding that the relator's claims against the owner defendants failed to allege scienter sufficiently. The court rejected the relator's argument that the owners' involvement in the industry and ownership of the steel company would have made obvious to them that the customs duties were not being paid. The court explained that the relator failed to allege that the owners were sufficiently experienced in the industry to grasp the customs violations, noting that the relator did not allege the owners' specific responsibilities or any information about the company's size or corporate structure, and thus alleged only scenarios in which the defendants possibly, rather than probably, possessed the required knowledge. The court also found that the relator failed to allege sufficiently that the owners were alter egos of the company.

JURISDICTIONAL ISSUES

A. Section 3730(b)(5) First-to-File Bar

U.S. ex rel. Zelickowski v. Albertsons LLC, 2018 WL 6609571 (W.D. Tex. Dec. 17, 2018)

> **Holding: The United States District Court for the Western District of Texas granted the defendant's motion to dismiss the relator's healthcare fraud claims pursuant to the first-to-file bar.**

The relator brought a *qui tam* action against the pharmacy where she was formerly employed, alleging that the defendant failed to charge the government the same deeply discounted rates for generic drugs that it charged to regular customers, thereby overcharging the government in violation of the False Claims Act. Another former employee had brought a case involving the same fraud scheme several months before the relator filed her complaint in November of 2015, and the earlier case was voluntarily dismissed in May of 2017. The relator filed an amended complaint in June of 2017, and the defendant moved to dismiss, arguing that the relator's claims were precluded by the first-to-file bar.

The court granted the defendant's motion to dismiss. The court considered the circuit split regarding whether the filing of an amended complaint could cure a first-to-file deficiency, and concluded that it could not. The court explained that the complaint was doomed at the time of filing and that dismissal was required under the language of the first-to-file bar.

U.S. ex rel. Bernier v. Infilaw Corp., 2018 WL 5839270 (M.D. Fla. Nov. 8, 2018)

> **Holding: The United States District Court for the Middle District of Florida granted the defendants' motion to dismiss the relator's education fraud claims, finding that the claims were precluded by the first-to-file bar, and in the alternative, failed to meet the pleading requirements of Rule 9(b).**

The relator brought a *qui tam* action against the law school where she was formerly employed and its parent company, alleging that the defendants violated the False Claims Act by accepting federal student loan funds without disclosing violations of their Program Participation Agreement (PPA) with the government. Specifically, the relator alleged that the defendants failed to uphold their obligation to serve as a fiduciary of the federal funds, failed to uphold their obligation to "develop, publish, administer, and enforce a code of conduct" with respect to the loans, and failed to implement a written plan to combat the unauthorized distribution of copyrighted material by users of the law school's network. She alleged that these were material obligations under the PPA, and that receiving the federal funds without disclosing the failure to meet these obligations violated the FCA. The defendants moved to dismiss, arguing that two previously-filed *qui tam* actions precluded the action under the first-to-file bar, and that relator failed to plead fraud with particularity under Rule 9(b).

The court granted the defendants' motion to dismiss on both grounds. The court found that two previously-filed actions precluded the relator's claims from going forward, explaining that while the earlier cases were filed against other subsidiary schools of the same parent company, the complaints sketch "the exact same fraudulent scheme]." The court noted that, while the details of relator's complaint differed in some respects, the complaints were "clearly related" under the first-to-file rule. Further, the court found that the relator's claims failed to meet the particularity requirements of Rule 9(b), explaining that the relator's claims were conclusory and vague and that she failed to plead that the certifications were actually false.

FALSE CLAIMS ACT RETALIATION CLAIMS

Brady v. Liquidity Serv., Inc., 2018 WL 6267766 (D.D.C. Nov. 30, 2018)

> **Holding: The United States District Court for the District of Columbia granted the defendant's motion to dismiss the plaintiff's retaliation claims.**

The plaintiff brought a retaliation claim under the False Claims Act against the government contractor where he was formerly employed, alleging that the defendant terminated his employment after he informed his supervisor and the company's CEO that they were required to share cost-saving information with the government. The plaintiff alleged that, as Vice President of Finance, he was required to develop new approaches to technology expenses, and that as part of this project he discovered ways to significantly cut technology costs. He alleged that he reported this to his supervisor and explained that they would have to share the cost-saving information with the government under the contract, and that it would be illegal not to tell the government about the cost-savings. After his supervisor indicated that they might not see eye to eye on his plan to share the information with the government, the plaintiff alleged that he reported it to the CEO, who told him "not to worry about it." He alleged that his employment was terminated shortly thereafter. The defendant moved to dismiss for failure to state a claim under Rule 12(b)(6).

The court granted the motion to dismiss, finding that the plaintiff was not engaged in protected activity. The court explained that the plaintiff's conduct could not have reasonably led to a viable FCA case because he reported only concerns about an impending violation, and did not allege that the violation actually took place or that the defendant took steps to commit a violation. The court also found that the plaintiff did not provide any facts showing that he engaged in activity outside of his normal job functions as Vice President of Finance.

Potts v. Ctr. for Excellence in Higher Educ., Inc., 908 F.3d 610 (10th Cir. Nov. 6, 2018)

> **Holding: The United States Court of Appeals for the Tenth Circuit upheld the district court's decision granting the defendant's motion to dismiss the plaintiff's retaliation claim, holding that the FCA's retaliation provision did not apply to post-employment conduct.**

The plaintiff brought a retaliation claim under the False Claims Act, alleging that the defendant non-profit college filed a state court lawsuit against her for purposes of harassment after she had filed a complaint with the defendant's accrediting agency. She had alleged that the defendant provided false information to the Department of Education in violation of the FCA, and that, after she resigned her employment due to the illegal practices, the defendant brought a retaliatory lawsuit alleging that she had violated the terms of her separation agreement. She argued that her complaint with the agency was protected activity under the FCA because it revealed violations of accreditation standards that would have disqualified the defendant from receiving federal funds. The United States District Court for the District of Colorado granted the defendant's motion to dismiss, finding that the FCA's retaliation provisions did not apply to post-employment conduct by a former employer. The plaintiff appealed to the Tenth Circuit.

The circuit court upheld the district court's decision, holding that the FCA "unambiguously excluded relief" for retaliatory acts occurring after an employee has left her job. The court explained that, based on its examination of the text of the statute, the FCA protected only current employees from retaliation. The court observed that four of the six qualifying retaliatory acts listed in the statute could by definition occur only during employment, and that the "associated-words canon" required it to construe the remaining qualifying acts as limited to current employment.

U.S. ex rel. Brumfield v. Narco Freedom, Inc., 2018 WL 5817379 (S.D.N.Y. Nov. 6, 2018)

Holding: The United States District Court for the Southern District of New York granted the defendant's motion to dismiss the relators' retaliation claims, holding that the retaliation provisions of the FCA did not apply to individual employers.

The relators brought a *qui tam* action against the non-profit corporation where they were formerly employed and against its Chief Executive Officer, Alan Brand, alleging that the defendants defrauded the government in violation of the False Claims Act. Five years later, the relators filed an amended complaint adding retaliation claims, alleging that they were fired as a result of their protected activity. Brand moved to dismiss the relators' retaliation claims for failure to state a claim under Rule 12(b)(6) and argued that the claims were time-barred.

The court granted Brand's motion to dismiss, finding that the FCA's retaliation provision did not allow suits to go forward against individual defendants. The court rejected the relators' argument that they were not bringing the suit against Brand in his individual capacity, but as an alter ego of the corporation, explaining that the relators failed to allege sufficient facts bearing on Brand's domination of the corporation or allegations that the corporate form was used as a fraud or sham. Alternatively, the court found that the retaliation claims were time-barred because they were not sufficiently set out in the original complaint and therefore the amended complaint did not relate back to the original.

See *U.S. ex rel. Gates v. United Airlines Inc.*, 912 F.3d 190 (4th Cir. Dec. 26, 2018)

See *U.S. ex rel. Pink v. Khan*, 2018 WL 5831222 (E.D. Pa. Nov. 7, 2018)

COMMON DEFENSES
TO FCA ALLEGATIONS

A. Failure to Prove Falsity

U.S. ex rel. Pink v. Khan, 2018 WL 5831222 (E.D. Pa. Nov. 7, 2018)

Holding: The United States District Court for the Eastern District of Pennsylvania granted the defendants' motion for summary judgment on the relators' Medicaid fraud claims, finding that the relator failed to provide evidence that the defendants actually submitted any false claims, but denied the defendants' motion for summary judgment on the relators' retaliation claims.

The relators brought a *qui tam* action against several healthcare service facilities, including Westfield Hospital and Lehigh Valley Pain Management (LVPM), the facilities' owners, and related consultants, alleging that the defendants violated the False Claims Act by engaging in a scheme to improperly bill Medicaid for uncovered services. The evidence showed that LVPM originally owned the defendants' MRI facility, but that the defendants transferred ownership of the facility to Westfield, and that LVPM continued to bill Medicaid for MRIs that were performed at the Westfield facility. The relators alleged that the defendants submitted factually false claims that misrepresented which healthcare entity provided the services, continuing to identify LVPM as the service provider. Further, they alleged that the defendants submitted legally false claims by impliedly certifying compliance with regulations for offsite hospital departments, which was no longer true after ownership of the MRI facility was transferred. The relators also alleged that they were fired after they raised concerns about the billing improprieties. The defendants moved for summary judgment.

The court granted the defendants' motion for summary judgment with respect to the substantive FCA claims. First, the court found that the relators failed to plead a factually false claim, explaining that continuing to submit bills for MRIs from LVPM after the facility was transferred to Westfield did not misrepresent what goods or services were provided. Rather, the court observed, the defendants "may have misrepresented the owner and operator of the facility providing the services," but this was not sufficient to state a valid claim because the government received what it paid for. Next, the court found that the relators' allegations of legal falsity failed because they did not provide any evidence of claims misrepresenting Westfield's compliance with regulations for offsite hospital departments or evidence of a single claim submitted by Westfield. Rather, they presented only evidence of claims submitted by LVPM, and failed to explain how those claims constituted a misrepresentation of LVPM's compliance with any relevant statute. The court explained that only a claim by Westfield could misrepresent Westfield's compliance with the offsite regulations. However, the court denied the defendants' motion for summary judgement on the relators' retaliation counts, explaining that the issues were fact-intensive and there were disputes of material fact as to the identity of the correct defendant in the retaliation claims.

FEDERAL RULES
OF CIVIL PROCEDURE

A. Rule 9(b) Failure to Plead Fraud with Particularity

U.S. ex rel. Benaissa v. Trinity Health, 2018 WL 6843624 (D.N.D. Dec. 31, 2018)

> **Holding: The United States District Court for the District of North Dakota granted the defendants' motion to dismiss the relator's Medicare fraud claims for failure to plead fraud with particularity under Rule 9(b). The court also granted the defendants' motion to dismiss the relator's retaliation allegations for failure to state a claim under Rule 12(b)(6).**

The relator brought a *qui tam* action against the hospital where he was formerly employed and its affiliates, alleging that the defendants violated the False Claims Act by falsely certifying that they were in compliance with the Anti-Kickback Statute and Stark Law while paying illegal kickbacks to and entering into illegal financial relationships with physicians in order to induce them to refer patients to the defendants' entities. He also alleged that doctors at the defendants' hospital were performing unnecessary surgeries and upcoding in order to overcharge Medicare. He included allegations specific to five patients for whom he alleged unnecessary surgeries were performed. The relator alleged that he informed his supervisors about the unnecessary surgeries and was subsequently terminated in violation of the FCA's retaliation provisions. The defendants moved to dismiss for failure to plead fraud with particularity under Rule 9(b) and failure to state a claim under Rule 12(b)(6).

The court granted the defendants' motion to dismiss, finding that the relator failed to plead his fraud claims with sufficient particularity. The court explained that the relator did not allege facts amounting to reliable indicia that false claims were actually submitted and failed to point to actual claims, rather than generally alleging that claims must have been submitted because the defendants received payments from Medicare. The court observed that the relator failed to link revenue received by the defendants to the submission of any claims for unnecessary surgeries or upcoding, and did not allege any personal knowledge of the defendants' billing practices. The court rejected the relator's argument that the defendants submitted false certifications in their annual cost reports, provider agreements, or forms seeking reimbursement from Medicare, and therefore every claim submitted was false, explaining that those allegations were not made with sufficient particularity because he did not identify specific agents who submitted the certificates, dates they were submitted, or any other details about the forms. The court also granted the defendants' motion to dismiss the relator's retaliation claims, finding that while he allegedly complained to his supervisors about unnecessary surgeries, he did not notify them that he was concerned that the defendants were committing fraud against the government.

U.S. ex rel. Headen v. Abundant Life Therapeutic Serv. Texas, LLC, 2018 WL 6266920 (S.D. Tex. Nov. 30, 2018)

Holding: The United States District Court for the Southern District of Texas granted the defendants' motion to dismiss the relator's kickback claims for failure to plead fraud with particularity under Rule 9(b).

The relator brought a *qui tam* action against the medical services provider where he was formerly employed and several other unnamed defendants, alleging that they paid kickbacks to schools, organizations, and physicians in order to generate patient referrals and submitted claims tainted by those kickbacks to the government in violation of the False Claims Act. The relator also alleged that the defendants submitted claims for medically unnecessary services to the government, employed physicians improperly, and provided illegal benefits to physicians. He alleged that the manager and director of the medical services provider told him about agreements with several schools under which the defendants would provide free services, donations, and other remuneration in exchange for student patient referrals. The defendants moved to dismiss for failure to plead fraud with particularity under Rule 9(b).

The court granted the defendants' motion, finding that the relator failed to plead the who, what, when, where, and how of the fraud. The court explained that the relator's kickback allegations were conclusory and did not tie any payments to the actual referral of patients. Where the relator did mention specific remuneration, the court observed that he failed to allege that any false claims were actually submitted as a result of those payments, or even whether the students ever received treatment. The court found that the remaining allegations regarding conspiracy, unnecessary claims, and improperly employed physicians were conclusory and vague.

U.S. ex rel. Juan v. Regents of Univ. of Ca., 2018 WL 6168529 (N.D. Ca. Nov. 26, 2018)

> **Holding: The United States District Court for the Northern District of California granted the defendants' motion to dismiss the relator's healthcare fraud claims with prejudice for failure to plead fraud with particularity under Rule 9(b).**

The relator brought a *qui tam* action against the regents of the University of California as a whole and against each individual regent alleging that they violated the False Claims Act by submitting fraudulent claims for Medicare and Medicaid services at the university. The individual defendants moved to dismiss for failure to plead fraud with particularity under Rule 9(b).

The court granted the motion to dismiss with prejudice. The court explained that the relator identified the defendants by name and job title once at the beginning of the complaint, but then improperly lumped all of the defendants together in pleading her claims throughout the complaint. The court found that the allegations were too vague and conclusory to satisfy Rule 9(b), and dismissed the claims with prejudice, noting that it had already granted leave to amend and fix the deficiencies in the complaint, but the relator had failed to do so and further amendment was futile.

U.S. ex rel. Capshaw v. White, 2018 WL 6068806 (N.D. Tex. Nov. 20, 2018)

> **Holding: The United States District Court for the Northern District of Texas denied the defendant's motion to dismiss the plaintiffs' kickback allegations for failure to plead fraud with particularity under Rule 9(b) and failure to state a claim under Rule 12(b)(6).**

In this partially intervened case, the relator brought a *qui tam* action against the owners of a hospice care provider, Bryan White and Suresh Kumar, alleging that the defendants conspired with a home care company to transfer money and equity to the company in exchange for the referral of patients to them for hospice care in violation of the Anti-Kickback Statute. The plaintiffs alleged that the defendants caused claims to be submitted to the government that were tainted by the kickback claims in violation of the False Claims Act. Kumar moved to dismiss for failure to state a claim under Rule 12(b)(6) and failure to plead fraud with particularity under Rule 9(b).

The court denied Kumar's motion to dismiss, finding that the plaintiffs had properly pled their claims. The court explained that the plaintiffs' complaint "painstakingly track[ed] the flow of loans to and referrals out of" the home care provider and the dates during which the fraud allegedly took place. The court also observed that the plaintiffs cited 30 different loans that the hospice care provider granted to the home care provider, and alleged that the defendants received over 70% of the home care provider's hospice patients. Further, the court noted that the plaintiffs alleged details of at least 24 specific patient referrals that led to at least 180 Medicare claims resulting from this relationship. The court also explained that the plaintiffs alleged that Kumar signed certifications that the hospice care provider was complying with the AKS while knowingly violating it. Finally, the court found that the plaintiffs sufficiently alleged materiality, explaining that the violations of the AKS were "serious, consequential, felony transgressions of law that the Government actively enforces."

See *U.S. ex rel. Gates v. United Airlines Inc.*, 912 F.3d 190 (4th Cir. Dec. 26, 2018)

See *U.S. ex rel. Mateski v. Raytheon Co.*, 745 Fed.Appx. 49 (9th Cir. Dec. 11, 2018)

See *U.S. ex rel. Hubert v. Bd. of Educ. of the City of Chicago*, 2018 WL 6248827 (N.D. Ill. Nov. 29, 2018)

See *U.S. ex rel. Streck v. Bristol-Myers Squibb Co.*, 2018 WL 6300578 (E.D. Pa. Nov. 29, 2018)

See *U.S. ex rel. Schagrin v. LDR Indus., LLC*, 2018 WL 6064699 (N.D. Ill. Nov. 20, 2018)

See *U.S. ex rel. Bernier v. Infilaw Corp.*, 2018 WL 5839270 (M.D. Fla. Nov. 8, 2018)

B. Rule 12(b)(6) Failure to State a Claim upon which Relief can be Granted

U.S. ex rel. Hubert v. Bd. of Educ. of the City of Chicago, 2018 WL 6248827 (N.D. Ill. Nov. 29, 2018)

> **Holding: The United States District Court for the Northern District of Illinois granted the defendants' motion to dismiss the relator's Medicaid fraud claims for failure to state a claim under Rule 12(b)(6) and failure to plead fraud with particularity under Rule 9(b).**

The relator, the former Director for Student Transportation Services for the Chicago Public School system, brought a *qui tam* action against the Board of Education for the City of Chicago (the Board) and several bus companies (the Vendors) with which the Board contracted to provide bus services for special needs students, alleging that the defendants conspired to overbill Medicaid for the transportation of special needs students in violation of the False Claims Act. The relator alleged that the Vendors colluded on contract prices during the competitive bidding process for their services in order to overcharge Medicaid. The relator also alleged that the Vendors submitted false invoices to the Board that included charges for services never actually rendered and students who never actually rode the bus, and that the Board knew the invoices were false, but submitted claims to the government for the services anyway. The defendants moved to dismiss for failure to state a claim under Rule 12(b)(6) and failure to plead fraud with particularity under Rule 9(b).

The court granted the defendants' motion to dismiss, rejecting the relator's request that the court relax the Rule 9(b) standard and finding that he failed to "plead his FCA claims 'at an individualized transaction level'" as required. The court explained that the relator did not sufficiently identify any individual from either the Board or the Vendors who actually submitted any false claims or show with particularity the actual requests for reimbursements that were allegedly submitted. Further, the court found that the relator did not allege what services were provided by which vendors, what certifications the Board made to the government, or what amounts were requested and paid. In addition, the court found that the relator did not sufficiently state a claim under Rule 12(b)(6), noting that he failed to show that the Board knew that the specific invoices the Vendors submitted were false, and observing that the allegations in the complaint repeatedly contradicted themselves as to what the defendants knew and when. The court also found that the relator failed to plead that the false statements were "so material that the Government would refuse payment were it aware of the violation."

U.S. ex rel. Streck v. Bristol-Myers Squibb Co., 2018 WL 6300578 (E.D. Pa. Nov. 29, 2018)

Holding: The United States District Court for the Eastern District of Pennsylvania denied the defendant's motion to dismiss the relator's Medicaid fraud claims for failure to state a claim under Rule 12(b)(6) and failure to plead fraud with particularity under Rule 9(b).

The relator, a pharmacist and former CEO of an association of prescription drug manufacturers, brought a *qui tam* action against a pharmaceutical manufacturer alleging that it fraudulently manipulated the calculation of Medicaid rebates it owed and underpaid the government in violation of the False Claims Act. He alleged that the defendant improperly characterized certain fees as "discount fees" rather than bona fide service fees in order to report a lower Average Manufacturer's Price (AMP) to Medicaid, thus lowering the rebate paid to Medicaid. The relator also alleged that the defendant underreported AMP by offsetting price increases against service fees owed to distributors in order to avoid including price increases in reported AMPs. The defendant moved to dismiss for failure to state a claim under Rule 12(b)(6) and failure to plead fraud with particularity under Rule 9(b).

The court denied the defendant's motion to dismiss, finding that the relator alleged sufficient facts to support his discount fee and service fee claims. First, the court found that the relator adequately alleged falsity, noting that the defendant's own consultant found that the fees were being improperly characterized and that the numbers reported to Medicaid were incorrect. The court found that the relator sufficiently alleged that the defendant's certifications that the AMP numbers were accurate were false. The court also observed that the defendant's practices were in direct conflict with CMS guidance, and that the relator properly alleged scienter by claiming that the guidance served to warn the defendant away from its erroneous interpretation of the regulations. Further, an opinion in an earlier case holding that the practices were improper also served as a "red flag" to warn the defendant to change its practices. The court rejected the defendant's argument that the violations were not material because the government decided not to intervene, noting that the government makes intervention decisions for various reasons not related to the merits of the case. The court found that the underreporting of AMP had the direct result of lowering the defendant's payment obligations, and that the misstatement of that data was material. The court also found that the relator adequately alleged that the defendant violated the reverse false claims provision of the FCA by underreporting the amount owed to Medicaid. Finally, the court found that the relator alleged his claims with sufficient particularity under Rule 9(b), explaining that he alleged detailed facts about when and how the schemes were carried out, and by whom.

See *U.S. ex rel. Benaissa v. Trinity Health*, 2018 WL 6843624 (D.N.D. Dec. 31, 2018)

See *U.S. ex rel. Capshaw v. White*, 2018 WL 6068806 (N.D. Tex. Nov. 20, 2018)

See *U.S. ex rel. Folliard v. Comstor Corp.*, 2018 WL 5777085 (D.D.C. Nov. 2, 2018)

LITIGATION DEVELOPMENTS

A. Costs and Attorneys' Fees

U.S. ex rel. Jacobs v. CDS, P.A., 2018 WL 6268201 (D. Id. Nov. 30, 2018)

> **Holding: The United States District Court for the District of Idaho granted the relator's motion for attorneys' fees, but reduced the total amount awarded for limited success.**

The relator brought a *qui tam* action against a healthcare provider and its affiliated alleging that the defendants violated the False Claims Act by falsely certifying compliance with the Anti-Kickback Statute and Stark Act. After the relator filed for bankruptcy, he and the government settled the claims with the relator's bankruptcy trustee for approximately $70,000. The relator then moved for attorneys' fees in the amount of approximately $106,000 and costs of approximately $1,130. The defendants opposed the motion, arguing that both the hourly rate and total hours awarded should be reduced.

The court granted the relator's motion for fees and costs, but reduced the total lodestar amount. The court rejected the defendants' argument that the hourly rate for the relator's attorneys was too high, explaining that it was a complex case and the attorneys had significant experience in complex litigation. The court also very slightly reduced the number of hours awarded due to vague time entries. Finally, because the plaintiff achieved limited success in the case in light of the much higher amount of damages he was seeking, the court reduced the lodestar amount by 20%.

B. Motion to Amend

U.S. ex rel. Bawduniak v. Biogen Idec, Inc., 2018 WL 5921641 (D. Mass. Nov. 13, 2018)

> **Holding: The United States District Court for the District of Massachusetts denied the relator's motion for leave to file an amended complaint, finding that the he acted with undue delay.**

The relator brought a *qui tam* action against biotechnology company Biogen Idec on behalf of the federal government and seventeen states, alleging that the defendant defrauded the federal government and the state-run Medicaid programs in violation of the False Claims Act. The court granted the defendant's motion to dismiss the state claims, finding that the relator failed to show that any false claims were submitted in individual states. The relator moved for leave to file an amended complaint, arguing that he had now received claims data from two states and was in the process of receiving additional data to supplement his claims.

The court denied the relator's motion, finding that he acted with undue delay in seeking the information necessary to amend his complaint. The court explained that it granted the defendant's motion to dismiss in July 2016, but that the relator did not make any effort to obtain the pertinent information until April 2018, and that this delay was unacceptable under the circumstances, as there was nothing preventing the relator from acting sooner.

C. Seal Issues

U.S. ex rel. Kammarayil v. Sterling Operations, Inc., 2018 WL 6839747 (D.D.C. Dec. 31, 2018)

> **Holding: The United States District Court for the District of Columbia granted the relators' motion for partial unsealing of the government's extension memoranda.**

The relators brought a *qui tam* action against the government contractor where they were formerly employed, alleging that the defendant conducted a "planned armed robbery" of its subcontractor, MAKS, Inc., and then submitted claims to the government for the loss of equipment that it had actually stolen. MAKS brought a successful civil lawsuit against the defendant for breach of contract and trespass, and the facts of that case stemmed from the same illegal activity alleged in the relators' subsequent *qui tam* action. The government sought seven seal extensions during the investigation into the *qui tam* allegations and, according to the relators, the government attorneys assigned to the case indicated that the government was likely going to intervene. When the government eventually declined intervention, the relators moved for partial unsealing of the government's extension memoranda in order to ascertain whether material discrepancies existed between the government's representations and its eventual declination, and whether the government had uncovered information that would help them decide whether they should continue to pursue the case. The government opposed the motion.

The court granted the relators' motion, rejecting the government's argument that the FCA "evinced the intent" to keep government extension memoranda under seal, explaining that the FCA was silent on the issue. The court also rejected the government's argument that unsealing the memoranda would disclose confidential investigative techniques and have a chilling effect on the drafting of future memoranda, explaining that the memoranda consist, for the most part, of boilerplate legal arguments and facts that are already in the public record, or at least already known to the relator. The court explained that investigatory efforts were described only in general terms and that the memoranda revealed no information that could be considered evaluative of the internal reasoning of the government. The court found that relators' surprise at the government's decision and their desire to find out whether the government had been untruthful with them throughout the investigation did not warrant unsealing on its own, but the fact that the memoranda might reveal a reason not to pursue their claims warranted partial unsealing as to relators.

Judgments & Settlements

NOVEMBER 1, 2018–DECEMBER 31, 2018

Compu-Link Corp. (M.D. Fla. Dec. 21, 2018)

Compu-Link Corporation (Celink) agreed to pay $4.25 million to resolve allegations that it obtained insurance payments for interest from Federal Housing Administration despite its failure to disclose that the mortgagee was ineligible for the payments. Celink, as a result, allegedly obtained additional interest that it was not entitled to. The investigation was led by the U.S. Attorney's Office with assistance from the Department of Housing and Urban Development Office of Inspector General.

Dr. Jonathan Daitch (M.D. Fla. Dec. 20, 2018)

Dr. Jonathan Daitch agreed to pay $1.718 million to the government to settle allegations that he received illegal kickbacks associated with anesthesia services and caused submission medically unnecessary urine tests. During the relevant period, Dr. Daitch was one of two principal owners of Advanced Pain Management Specialists, P.A. The other principal owner, Dr. Michael Frey, previously pleaded guilty to two counts of conspiracy to receive illegal kickbacks and agreed to a civil settlement for $2.8 million. The two doctors also owned Anesthesia Partners of SWFL, LLC that provided anesthesia services exclusively for the procedures performed by the Advanced Pain physicians. The complaint alleged that the arrangement resulted in improper remuneration to Dr. Daitch as an owner and his ownership interest and the received remuneration induced him to refer his patients for anesthesia services to Anesthesia Partners. In addition to the civil settlement, Dr. Daitch, Advanced Pain, and Park Center for Procedures—an ambulatory surgical center owned by Daitch and Frey—entered into a five-year Corporate Integrity Agreement with the Office of Inspector General of the United States Department of Health and Human Services.

Dr. Irfan Siddiqui and Heart and Vascular Institute of Florida (M.D. Fla. Dec. 19, 2018)

Dr. Irfan Siddiqui and his vascular surgery practice, Heart and Vascular Institute of Florida (HAVI) agreed to pay the government $2,230,000 to settle allegations that they submitted false claims to federal health programs for reimbursement on vein ablation services. The services were allegedly medically unnecessary or performed by unqualified personnel or both. They allegedly up-coded evaluation and management service claims to levels of service that were not supported by medical records as well. One of his patients brought a *qui tam* lawsuit raised initial allegations, and the whistleblower will receive $446,000 as his share.

Molecular Testing Labs (W.D. Wash. Dec. 19, 2018)

Molecular Testing Labs, a subsidiary of Blackfly Investments, LLC, agreed to pay $1,777,738 to resolve allegations that it paid illegal kickbacks to local laboratories for referrals from government healthcare insurance programs. Molecular Testing Labs then allegedly used illegal referrals to submit claims for payment to federal healthcare programs. Molecular Testing Labs remains in separate litigation with the Centers for Medicare & Medicaid Services regarding potential claims overpayment.

SouthernCare, Inc. (E.D. Pa. Dec. 13, 2018)

SouthernCare, Inc. a hospice care service, agreed to pay $5,863,426 to settle allegations that the company submitted claims to Medicare for hospice care that was medically unnecessary or lacked documentation. Two separate *qui tam* lawsuits filed by former employees of SouthernCare raised initial allegations, and the relators will share approximately $1.1 million of the recovery.

Finance of America Mortgage LLC (N.D. N.Y. Dec. 12, 2018)

Finance of America Mortgage LLC agreed to pay the government $14,500,000 to resolve allegations that its acquired company, Gateway Funding Diversified Mortgage Services L.P. (Gateway), knowingly originated and underwrote deficient mortgage loans insured by the U.S. Department of Housing and Urban Development's (HUD) Federal Housing Administration (FHA). As part of the settlement, Gateway admitted that it failed to audit all early-payment default loans (EPD) as required by HUD and ignored warnings from its compliance department regarding the company's poor EPD rate for FHA loans. It also admitted that it failed to adhere to HUD's self-reporting requirements for loans containing material deficiencies. A *qui tam* lawsuit triggered the government investigation, and the whistleblower, a former Gateway employee, will receive $2,392,500 of the settlement.

Aurora Health Care Inc. (E.D. Wis. Dec. 11, 2018)

Aurora Health Care, Inc. (Aurora) agreed to pay $12 million to the United States and the State of Wisconsin to resolve allegations that Aurora submitted claims to Medicare and Medicaid in violation of the Stark Law. The government alleged that Aurora entered into compensation arrangements, which were not commercially reasonable and exceeded the fair market value of the physicians' services, with two physicians. The allegations resulted from a whistleblower lawsuit. The whistleblowers' complaint alleged different claims that were not the basis for this settlement. The United States and the State of Wisconsin are not intervening in pursuing those claims. As part of the settlement, the United States, the State of Wisconsin, and the whistleblowers asked the district court to dismiss the *qui tam* complaint.

Benjamin D. George, Jody C. Rookstool, Western Medical Group (D. Utah Dec. 11, 2018)

Benjamin D. George, Jody C. Rookstool, and their company, Western Medical Group, agreed to pay approximately $1.6 million to resolve allegations that the company caused the submission of false claims to Medicare and violated Medicare's prohibition against telephone solicitation of covered products to beneficiaries. The settlement resolves allegations originally brought by two *qui tam* actions.

Coordinated Health Holding Co., LLC and Emil DiIorio, M.D. (E.D. Pa. Dec. 11, 2018)

Coordinated Health Holding Company, LLC (Coordinated Health) and Emil DiIorio, M.D., the company's founder, principal owner, and CEO, reached a settlement agreement with the government to resolve allegations under the FCA with the total payment of $12.5 million. Coordinated Health agreed to pay $11.25 million and Dr. DiIorio agreed to pay $1.25 million. They allegedly submitted false claims to federal health care programs, including Medicare, for orthopedic surgeries. The government alleged that Coordinated Health and Dr. DiIorio improperly unbundled claims for surgery reimbursements to inflate reimbursements. It is improper "unbundling" when a provider submits a claim for a global reimbursement for a surgery and misuses billing codes to separately bill parts of the same surgery. Coordinated Health was informed several times on the misuse of billing codes. The claims resolved by the settlement were allegations only. There was no determination of liability.

Oviatt Hearing and Balance, LLC (N.D. N.Y. Dec. 11, 2018)

Oviatt Hearing and Balance, LLC (Oviatt) agreed to pay $566,263.08 to resolve false claims allegations that it billed the federal government for services rendered by unlicensed individuals and inappropriately provided gift cards and other inducements to Medicare and TRICARE beneficiaries. As part of the settlement, Oviatt admitted both allegations. A *qui tam* lawsuit triggered the investigation, and the relator will receive $120,000 of the settlement proceeds.

Target Corp. (D. Minn. Dec. 11, 2018)

Target Corporation agreed to pay $3,000,000 to resolve allegations that it violated the federal FCA and Massachusetts FCA by submitting claims for payment to Massachusetts' Medicaid program (MassHealth) in violation of prohibiting Medicaid prescriptions from being automatically refiled. Target allegedly knowingly and routinely enrolled MassHealth beneficiaries in the auto-refill program and billed MassHealth for prescriptions until it sold its pharmacy business to CVS Health. The settlement resolves allegations initially brought by a whistleblower.

M. Wagdi Attia, M.D. (D. Md. Dec. 7, 2018)

M. Wagdi Attia, M.D., agreed to pay $400,000 to resolve allegations that he fraudulently billed Medicare and Medicaid for services that were not rendered. Furthermore, Dr. Attia agreed to retire from the medical practice, to allow his medical license to expire, to allow his Medicare and Medicaid billing privileges to lapse. He showed no intention to renew his license or Medicare/Medicaid privileges.

Actelion Pharmaceuticals US, Inc. (D. Mass. Dec. 6, 2018)

Actelion, a San Francisco-based pharmaceutical company, agreed to pay $360 million to resolve claims that it violated the FCA by illegally using a foundation as a pipeline to pay the copays of Medicare patients taking its drugs. The government alleged that used data obtained from the foundation on how much the foundation had spent for patients on each drug to decide how much to donate to the foundation and to confirm that its contributions were enough to cover the copays of only patients taking the drugs. Actelion allegedly engaged in the practice even though the foundation had warned the company against receiving the data. The claims resolved by the settlement were allegations only, and there was no determination of liability.

Anil J. Desai, M.D., East Metro Internal Medicine, LLC, and Rockdale-Newton Hematology-Oncology (N.D. Ga. Dec. 5, 2018)

Anil J. Desai, M.D. and his companies, East Metro Internal Medicine, LLC, and Rockdale-Newton Hematology-Oncology (the Desai Parties,) agreed to pay $213,000 to resolve allegations that they submitted claims to Medicare and Medicaid for drugs that were never provided to their patients, and for drugs that had not received final marketing approval by the Food and Drug Administration. The case was investigated by the U.S. Attorney's Office for the Northern District of Georgia, the Department of Health and Human Services – Office of Inspector General, and the Food and Drug Administration – Office of Criminal Investigations.

ev3 Inc., Covidien LP (D. Mass., C.D. Cal. Dec. 4, 2018)

A medical manufacturer ev3 Inc. agreed to plead guilty to charges concerning its neurovascular medical device and pay $17.9 million. Covidien LP, whose parent acquired ev3, separately paid $13 million to resolve the FCA allegations of payment of kickbacks in connection with another medical device. Despite the U.S. Food and Drug Administration's (FDA) limited approval of the medical device, ev3 sales representatives encouraged surgeons to use the device in large quantities for unproven and potentially dangerous surgical uses outside of the approved scope. The representatives attended surgical procedures and even provided explicit instructions on how to use the device for unapproved surgical procedures. Covidien allegedly paid kickbacks to promote the use of its Solitaire mechanical thrombectomy device. The government alleged that Covidien paid kickbacks to hospitals and institutions and caused false claims submitted to Medicare and Medicaid.

Rosicki, Rosicki & Associates, P.C. (S.D. N.Y. Dec. 4, 2018)

A New York law firm, Rosicki, Rosicki & Associates, P.C. (Rosicki) and its wholly-owned affiliates, Enterprise Process Service, Inc. (Enterprise) and Paramount Land, Inc. (Paramount) agreed to pay more than $6 million to resolve claims that they violated the False Claims Act. They allegedly generated false and inflated bills for foreclosure-related and eviction-related expenses and caused the expenses to be submitted to and paid by the Federal National Mortgage Association (Fannie Mae). The settlement resolves claims arising from misconduct in connection with eviction-related expenses that were submitted to and paid for by the U.S. Department of Veterans Affairs. As part of the settlement, the defendants admitted and agreed to pay $4.6 million to the United States. Rosicki must implement a compliance program with regular reporting over the next five years and to publicly disclose the nature of its affiliation with Enterprise and Paramount on its website. A *qui tam* lawsuit triggered the investigation. In March 2018, the United States intervened in the case. As part of a separate settlement, Rosicki, Enterprise, and Paramount agreed to pay the United States an additional $1,518,000 to resolve separate FCA violation claims pursued by the whistleblower.

SK Energy Co. Ltd., GS Caltex Corp., Hanjin Transportation Co. Ltd. (S.D. Ohio Nov. 14, 2018)

Three South Korea-based companies agreed to plead guilty to criminal charges and pay a total of approximately $82 million in criminal fines for their role in a decade-long bid-rigging conspiracy that targeted contracts to supply fuel to the U.S. Army, Navy, Marine Corps, and Air Force based in South Korea. The government argued that such action is a violation of Section4A of the Clayton Act. In separate civil resolutions, the companies agreed to pay a total of approximately $154 million to the government for civil antitrust and FCA violations. A *qui tam* lawsuit led to the government's FCA civil investigation.

Shaw University (E.D. N.C. Nov. 12, 2018)

Shaw University and local contractor Freddy Novelo agreed to pay $316,900 to resolve allegations that a former Shaw University official and a local building contractor made false statements and violated competitive bid requirements to obtain Department of Education grant funds, violating the FCA. The allegations resolved by the settlement were raised in a *qui tam* lawsuit.

British Airways and Iberia Airlines (Nov. 12, 2018)

British Airways Plc (BA) and Iberia Airlines (Iberia) agreed to pay $5.8 million to resolve their liability under the FCA. BA and Iberia allegedly falsely reported the times the airlines transferred U.S. mail to foreign postal administrations or other intended recipients under contracts with the United States Postal Service (USPS). The investigation was led by the Department of Justice's Civil Division, the USPS Office of the Inspector General, and the USPS Office of General Counsel.

Dandrow's Painting, Inc. (N.D. N.Y. Nov. 7, 2018)

Dandrow's Painting, Inc. agreed to pay $350,000 to resolve allegations that it failed to purchase and apply sufficient quantities of a penetrating sealing agent to meet its obligations under federally funded contracts. If a sufficient amount of the sealant is not applied, the bridge deck might not be protected against weather-related deterioration. The U.S. Attorney's Office for the Northern District of New York, the U.S. Department of Transportation—Office of Inspector General, the New York State – Inspector General, and the New York State Department of Transportation led the investigation and the settlement.

Maryland Treatment Centers (D. M.D. Nov. 7, 2018)

Maryland Treatment Centers reached a settlement to pay the United States $500,000 to settle allegations that it violated the FCA by submitting false claims for mental health and substance abuse services that were undocumented or not provided. Specifically, Maryland Treatment Centers submitted claims for services for which Maryland Treatment Centers failed to document. The settlement resolved a *qui tam* lawsuit. The whistleblower will receive $75,000 from the settlement.

ImmediaDent of Indiana, LLC (W.D. Ky. Nov. 6, 2018)

ImmediaDent of Indiana, LLC (ImmediaDent) and Samson Dental Partners (SDP), which provides administrative support services to ImmediaDent, agreed to pay the federal and state governments $5.139 million to resolve allegations that they improperly billed Indiana's Medicaid program for dental services. Specifically, the companies allegedly improperly billed simple tooth extractions as surgical extractions and improperly billed Scale and Root Plannings that were either not performed or not medically necessary. The settlement resolves allegations from a *qui tam* suit filed by Dr. Jihaad Abdul-Majid.

Northrop Grumman Systems Corporation (S.D. Cal. Nov. 2, 2018)

Northrop Grumman Systems Corporation (NGSC) agreed to settle civil allegations of violation of the FCA by overstating the number of hours its employees worked on two battlefield communications contract with the U.S. Air Force. NGSC agreed to pay $25.8 million. Combined with earlier repayments, the civil recovery resulted in approximately $27.45 million. NGSC additionally entered into a separate agreement with the Criminal Division of the U.S. Attorney's Office for the Southern District of California and agreed to forfeit an additional $4.2 million. Excluding the conduct admitted in the criminal agreement, the claims resolved by the civil agreement were allegations only, and there was no determination of civil liability.

Made in the USA
Monee, IL
13 January 2022

88830193R00031